There Is A Plan

ZONDERVAN®

There Is a Plan
Copyright © 2009 by Ravi Zacharias

Requests for information should be addressed to:

Zondervan, *Grand Rapids, Michigan 49530*

ISBN 978-0-310-31849-1

Content excerpted from *The Grand Weaver* by Ravi Zacharias. Copyright © 2007, Zondervan. Used by permission.

All Scripture quotations, unless otherwise indicated, are taken from the *Holy Bible, New International Version®*, NIV Copyright © 1973, 1978, 1984 by International Bible Society. Used by permission of Zondervan. All rights reserved.

Interior design by Melissa Elenbaas

Printed in China

09 10 11 12 • 4 3 2 1

Content in this book excerpted from
The Grand Weaver by Ravi Zacharias.

God Has Plans For You

The LORD will fulfill his purpose for me; your love, O LORD, endures forever—do not abandon the works of your hands.

Psalm 138:8

We know that in all things God works for the good of those who love him, who have been called according to his purpose.

Romans 8:28

We are God's workmanship, created in Christ Jesus to do good works, which God prepared in advance for us to do.

Ephesians 2:10

All of us experience sudden disappointment and unexpected events. And when something terrible happens we often declare, "That's life!"—as though disappointment and heartache declare the sum total of this existence.

We miss the roses and see only the thorns. We take for granted the warmth of the sun and get depressed by the frequency of the rain or the snow. We ignore the sounds of life in a nursery because we are preoccupied with the sounds of sirens responding to an emergency.

Yet God has a specific purpose for each of us and he will carry us through. However, recognizing that plan is not a simple thing. Our journey cannot be one only of unmistakable blessing and a path of ease. To allow God to be God we must follow him for who he is and what he intends, and not for what we want or what we prefer.

A Tender Heart

In order to see God's pattern in your life, you must develop a tender heart.

Jesus said, "You are the ones who justify yourselves in the eyes of men, but God knows your hearts."

Luke 16:15

Today, if you hear his voice, do not harden your hearts.

Hebrews 3: 7-8

Therefore, since we have a great high priest who has gone through the heavens, Jesus the Son of God, let us hold firmly to the faith we profess. For we do not have a high priest who is unable to sympathize with our weaknesses, but we have one who has been tempted in every way, just as we are.

Hebrews 4:14-15

At the end of your life one of three things will happen to your heart: it will grow hard, it will be broken, or it will be tender. Nobody escapes. Your heart will become coarse and desensitized, be crushed under the weight of disappointment, or be made tender by that which makes the heart of God tender as well. God's heart is a caring heart.

God seeks those with tender hearts so that he can put his imprint on them. Your hurts and your disappointments are part of that design, to shape your heart and the way you feel about reality. The hurts you live through will always shape you. There is no other way.

A Mind Of Faith

Do not conform any longer to the pattern of this world, but be transformed by the renewing of your mind. Then you will be able to test and approve what God's will is—his good, pleasing and perfect will.

Romans 12:2

*Because he himself suffered when he was tempted,
he is able to help those who are being tempted.*
Hebrews 2:18

I say to myself, "The LORD is my portion, therefore I will wait for him. The LORD is good to those whose hope is in him, to the one who seeks him; it is good to wait quietly for the salvation of the LORD.

Lamentations 3:24-26

In order to see God's pattern in your life, you must have a mind of faith. What the brain is to the body, the mind is to the soul. If you do not believe that God is in control and has formed you for a purpose, then you will flounder on the high seas of purposelessness, drowning in the currents and drifting further into nothingness.

Yet, we don't want to believe God is in control. We think that if only we were in control, everything would be fine. I have a friend who is terrified of flying because, he says, he cannot handle anything that he cannot control. I did not want to offend him by saying, "Welcome to life." God has made it imperative in the design of life that we become willing to trust beyond ourselves. Walking by faith means to follow someone else who knows more than we do, someone who is also good.

The love of God shows us that God alone bridges the distance between him and us, enabling us to see this world through Calvary. If you don't see it that way, then you will never see it his way—and the threads of the masterpiece he is weaving of your life will always pull away from the design.

Find God's Calling

If the LORD delights in a man's way, he makes his steps firm; though he stumble, he will not fall, for the LORD upholds him with his hand.

Psalm 37:23-34

Trust in the Lord with all your heart and lean not on your own understanding; in all your ways acknowledge him, and he will make your paths straight.

Proverbs 3: 5-6

I will lead the blind by ways they have not known, along unfamiliar paths I will guide them; I will turn the darkness into light before them and make the rough places smooth. These are the things I will do; I will not forsake them.

Isaiah 42:16

We all seek success, eager to grab whatever we can along the way. Yet accomplishment and dream careers do not necessarily lead to happiness. Making it to number one really means knowing where God wants you to be and serving him there with your best efforts. The goal is to find the threads God has in place for you and to follow his plan for you with excellence.

God, in his extraordinary way, can bring failure to you or cast you into prison in order to help you find your true calling. A calling is simply God's shaping of your burden and beckoning you to your service to him in the place and pursuit of his choosing.

A call may not necessarily feel attractive to you, but it will tug on your soul in an inescapable way, no matter how high the cost of following it may be. Finding that call gives you that hand-in-glove sensation and provides the security of knowing that you are utilizing your gifts and your will to God's ends first, not yours.

The drive to become number one is often the very thing that ultimately destroys a person. It simply cannot deliver the fulfillment we seek. Story after story bears this out.

Some time ago, I read about former New York Mets pitcher Dwight Gooden. He is serving a prison term for parole violation following a cocaine offense. Gooden was rookie of the year in 1984 and a Cy Young award winner in 1985. What more could a Major League pitcher want in his first two years on the mound? He had one more goal. In 1986 the Mets won the World Series in a spectacular, come-from-behind win over the Red Sox. Gooden was a member of that team. The championship capped a storybook sequence of his first three years in the majors.

Now in prison, Gooden looks back on that championship year with a broken heart and shattered dreams. He remembers not his feelings of ecstasy in becoming a "world champion," but that it was then that he began his flirtation with cocaine. From that time on, his career spiraled down until it had vanished.

It would be nice if all of us could be number one; it's just not possible or realistic. Somebody has to be number two—and number three and four, and on down the line. The drive to become number one is often the very thing that ultimately destroys a person. It simply cannot deliver the fulfillment we seek.

God often calls us to things that don't make sense to us. Some come to their calling through winding paths, some through the nicely paved road of privileged birth or influential friends. Others come through the visitation of circumstances with wanderings and sudden signposts. Finding one's calling is one of the greatest challenges of life, especially when one has gifts that fan out in many directions.

Fortunately, the Christian walk is not a clueless journey that begins with conversion and ends with heaven, while we mark time in between. No, God has designed us to work for his honor. He has intricately woven together my hopes, my dreams, and my vocation. God's plan for each one of us includes the way he has wired our thinking and has prepared whatever it is in our lives that will bring us fulfillment. Though we all want to determine our exact calling quickly, God reveals the particulars against a general backdrop.

Our first general calling is to understand God's primary description of who and what we are.

Some time ago, I attended a Bible study session with some sports professionals. The speaker that morning challenged the players to leave a legacy they could be proud of. He began by asking them how many knew the name of their great-grandfather. A few hands went up. Then he asked how many of them knew where their great-grandfather was buried. Most of the hands stayed down. With each more specific question, fewer hands went up.

He then made his point: "Each one of us is just three to four generations away from extinction." Silence gripped the room. How sobering to think that, just a few generations down the family tree, no one would even know I had ever existed! Then the speaker challenged these men about the legacy they would leave behind. One after another, the players responded.

But then one said, "Really, I don't care whether or not my great-great-grandson or great-granddaughter knows that I played ball professionally. It really doesn't matter that much. I just want them to know the God I served and loved." The words came from the heart.

Submit to God's design, and be number one in his eyes.

Know that you are God's temple.

Bathe your life in prayer.

Live out your life in humility of spirit that serves for the right reasons.

Seek the counsel and example of godly men and women.

Exhibit a commitment to the pre-eminence of Christ in all things.

Self-glory, power, sensuality, and the seduction of material gain impede a call.

Do The Right Thing

Jesus said, "Let your light shine before men, that they may see your good deeds and praise your Father in heaven. "

Matthew 5:16

So whether you eat or drink or whatever you do, do it all for the glory of God.

I Corinthians 10:31

It is the LORD your God you must follow, and him you must revere. Keep his commands and obey him, serve him and hold fast to him.

Deuteronomy 13:4

Jesus said; "Blessed rather are those who hear the word of God and obey it."

Luke 11:28

While at a conference in another country, I was approached by a young woman, who asked if she could talk to me privately. Once we found a couple of chairs and sat down to talk, I learned that she was miles away from the land of her birth and had lived through some horrendous experiences.

She had a beautiful mother, but her father, as she worded it, did not have the same admirable looks. Through an arranged marriage, they had begun their lives together, but the father always resented his wife's looks and the many compliments given to her, while none ever came his way. His distorted thinking took him beyond jealousy to fears that some man might lure her away, and so he made his plan to snuff out any such possibility. One day, he returned home, and while talking to his wife in their bedroom he reached into his bag, grabbed a bottle of acid, and flung the contents into her face. In one instant, he turned his wife's face from beautiful to horrendously scarred. He then turned and fled from the house.

At the point of our conversation two decades had gone by since mother and daughter had last seen him. The young woman, now in her twenties, had been a little girl when this tragic event took place, and yet the bitterness in her heart remained as fresh as the day she saw her mother's face turned from beauty to ugliness—so hideous that it forced the little one to cover her own face so she wouldn't have to see what had been done.

But the story did not end there. Just a few days before our conversation, the mother, who had raised the family on her own, had heard from the husband who had deserted her. He was dying of cancer and living alone. He wondered if she would take him back and care for him in this last stage of his illness. The audacious plea outraged this young woman. But the mother, a devout follower of Jesus Christ, pleaded with her children to let her take him back and care for him as he prepared to die.

In this story we see all the elements of the human fall and the power of a redeemed heart. Morality alone would dictate that he gets what he deserves. A redeemed heart says, "Let me bind his wounds because what needs attention is his soul."

Whatever you do, whether it be at work or in marriage, through your language or your ambitions, in your thoughts or your intents, do all and think all to the glory of God and by the rules he has put in place—rules that serve not to restrain us but to be the means for us to soar with the purpose for which he has designed all choices.

Choose To Live
Within God's Will

Do not let anyone lead you astray. He who does what is right is righteous, just as God is righteous.
I John 3:7

In the way of righteousness there is life; along that path is immortality.

Proverbs 12:28

The world and its desires pass away, but the man who does the will of God lives forever.

I John 2:17

Be joyful always; pray continually; give thanks in all circumstances, for this is God's will for you in Christ Jesus.

I Thessalonians 5:16-18

For it is God who works in you to will and to act according to his good purpose.

Philippians 2:13

Choose for yourselves this day whom you will serve . . .

Joshua 24:15

God has created a free will in each one of us. In order to realize God's plan for our lives, we must make choices in accordance with his will. God puts opportunities for us to do the "right" thing before us in many ways.

In September 1985, Reader's Digest ran a story titled "Letter in the Wallet," written by Arnold Fine. Fine tells how one bitterly cold day he stumbled upon a wallet on the street. It had just three dollars in it and a crumpled-up letter that obviously had been carried around for many years. The letter was dated sixty years earlier and began, "Dear Michael." The beautifully written, sadly worded letter ended a romance because of a parent's demands. The last line promised, "I will always love you, Michael," and was signed, "Yours, Hannah."

Fine decided to try to track down the owner of the wallet. Using Hannah's address, still legible on the letter, he finally retrieved a telephone number. But when he called it, he was disappointed (though not surprised) to learn that Hannah and her family had long ago moved out of the house. The person on the other end of the line, however, knew the name of the nursing home to which Hannah's mother had gone. So Fine called the nursing home and learned that Hannah's mother was no longer living. When he told them what he was trying to do, however, they gave him the address and telephone number they had on file for Hannah. He called the number and found out that Hannah herself now lived in a nursing home. Fine asked for the name of the home and found the phone number. Soon he was able to confirm that, yes, Hannah was a resident there. As soon as he could, Fine decided to visit the nursing home and try to talk with Hannah.

The director met him at the door and told him that Hannah was watching television on the third floor. An escort quickly took Fine there and then left. Fine introduced himself to Hannah and explained how he had found a letter in a wallet. He showed her the letter and asked if she was the one who had written it.

"Yes," Hannah replied. "I sent this letter to Michael because I was only sixteen and my mother wouldn't let us see each other anymore. He was very handsome, you know, like Sean Connery." Fine could see both the twinkle in her eye and the joy on her face as she spoke of her love for Michael. "Yes, Michael Goldstein was his name. If you find him, tell him that I think of him often and never did marry anyone. No one ever matched up to him," she declared, discreetly brushing tears from her eyes. Fine thanked her for her time and left.

As Mr. Fine was leaving the home, the security guard at the door asked him about his visit. He told the story and said, "At least I was able to get the last name from her. His name is Michael Goldstein."

"Goldstein?" repeated the guard. "There's a Mike Goldstein who lives here on the eighth floor." Fine turned around and went back inside, this time to the eighth floor, where he asked for Michael Goldstein. When directed to an elderly gentleman, he asked the man, "Have you lost your wallet?"

"Oh, yes, I lost it when I was out for a walk the other day," Michael answered.

Fine handed him the wallet and asked if it was his. Michael was delighted to see it again, and, full of gratitude to the finder, proceeded to thank him for returning it when Fine interrupted him.

"I have something to tell you," Fine admitted. "I read the letter in your wallet."

Caught off guard, Michael paused for a moment and then asked, "You read the letter?"

"Yes, sir, and I have further news for you," Fine continued. "I think I know where Hannah is."

Michael grew pale. "You know where she is? How is she?"

"She's fine, and just as pretty as when you knew her."

"Could you tell me where she is? I'd love to call her. You know, when that letter came to me, my life ended. I've never gotten married. I never stopped loving her."

"Come with me," said Fine. He took Michael by the elbow and led him to the elevator and down to the third floor. By this time, the director of the building had rejoined them. They came to Hannah's room.

"Hannah," the director whispered, gesturing toward Michael, "Do you know this man?"

She adjusted her glasses and looked at the man as she searched her memory bank. Then with a choked voice, Michael spoke up, "Hannah, it's Michael." She stood as he walked over to her. They embraced and held onto each other for as long as they could stay steady on their feet. They sat down, holding hands, and between their tears they filled in the story of the long years that had passed. Feeling as though they had intruded on a sacred moment, Mr. Fine and the director slowly slipped away to leave the two alone to enjoy their reunion.

Three weeks later, Arnold Fine received an invitation to attend the wedding of Hannah, seventy-six years of age, and Michael, seventy-eight. Fine closes his story by saying, "How good the work of the Lord is."

Such a touching story can make one believe that it had to have been made in heaven. But think about it. Made in heaven it could be; the work of a sovereign God leaves all of us overwhelmed at the way God weaves threads. At the same time, three determined wills all played a role here. A man loved his girl so much that he stayed faithful to her and remained single his whole life because he could not love another woman in this same way. A woman remained true to her first love, though she had been just a teen-ager, and she committed to honoring her parents' wishes. A man had resolved to return a wallet because he thought a poignant little letter kept for six decades merited a determined search for the owner.

The will is a strong but fragile part of every human life and it matters in the rich weaving of your life's tapestry that is in the making.

Finding The Sacred
In The Everyday

The heavens declare the glory of God; the skies proclaim the work of his hands.

Psalm 19:1

So whether you eat or drink or whatever you do, do it all for the glory of God.

I Corinthians 10:31

Jesus said, "Look at the birds of the air; they do not sow or reap or store away in barns, and yet your heavenly Father feeds them."

Matthew 6:26

Culture finds its most sublime and supreme expression when humanity focuses on God instead of themselves. Let me illustrate with a real-life example.

I had just finished lecturing on "Man's Search for Meaning." A student stood up and shouted at me, "Everything in life in meaningless!" We exchanged line for line, and he always came back with the same retort: "Everything in life is meaningless!" Finally I assured him that he could not possibly mean it, for the simple reason that I assumed that he assumed that what he was saying was meaningful—and if what he was saying was meaningful, then everything is not meaningless. On the other hand, if everything was meaningless, what he had just said was meaningless too, and therefore, in effect, he had said nothing.

After a short, pin-drop silence, the audience burst into laughter—an unfortunate response for this student. As I walked out of the auditorium, I still remember so clearly seeing him muttering to himself, repeating my words, "If everything is meaningless, then what I said is meaningless; on the other hand. . ." I must admit that I found it a humorous sight.

But something special happened later that night. I spoke at a local church in front of a packed house. At the close of the message, I invited men and women to come to the altar and kneel if they wanted to become followers of Jesus Christ. The first to stand and make his way forward was that same young man who earlier in the day had questioned the very possibility that anything had meaning. I stepped away from the pulpit and knelt beside him. In a strange way, he commented, his questions had betrayed his hunger for meaning. Kneeling now at the altar, he recognized that in the act of submission and worship, even his questions were justified.

Whether we seek ways to find pleasure or answers to the questions of a troubled mind, the solution begins with a willingness to see the sacredness of all of life. It must begin by making life an altar—and at an altar we had dare not lie. It is there that life recognizes the sacred.

Finding Your Destiny

"For I know the plans I have for you," declares the LORD, "plans to prosper you and not to harm you, plans to give you hope and a future. Then you will call upon me and come and pray to me, and I will listen to you. You will seek me and find me when you seek me with all your heart. I will be found by you," declares the LORD.

Jeremiah 29:11-14

We are children of God, and what we will be has not yet been made known. But we know that when he appears, we shall be like him, for we shall see him as he is.

I John 3:2

Listen, you who say, "Today or tomorrow we will go to this or that city, spend a year there, carry on business and make money." Why, you do not even know what will happen tomorrow . . . Instead, you ought to say, "If it is the Lord's will, we will live and do this or that. "

James 4:13-15

I had a very close friend in my undergraduate days named Koos Fietje—a tall and determined Dutchman, a man with a tender heart and a fearless personality. We shared many hours of friendship and conversation.

Eventually, he and his wife, Colleen, served as missionaries in Thailand. On one occasion while en route to Cambodia, I stopped for a night in Bangkok, and Koos and I talked the whole night long about our dreams and plans to work for God wherever he led us and called us. We prayed together, and after we parted, I could not stop thinking about what Koos had said to me. He felt he would have to pay with his life for his boldness for Christ. Seven years after that conversation, in 1981, Koos Fietje was murdered in the little town in Thailand where he had proclaimed Christ so fearlessly.

More than twenty years went by before I met his daughter, Martina, for the first time. She had come to one of my lectures and had been standing nearby while others took their turn to speak with me for a little while. She then introduced herself. "I've been waiting a long time to meet you," she said, "because I was told that you were one of my dad's closest friends."

I put my arm around her, and we sat down to talk. She was very little when her father was killed and had never returned to Thailand. She was now a young married woman, but she still felt haunted by memories of her father's death. She wished that some day she could visit his grave in Thailand. I took it upon myself to make her wish come true, and recently our ministry sent Martina and her husband to Thailand. When she returned, she wrote these words to me:

Dear Ravi,

Dave and I returned from Thailand this week and are overwhelmed by God's graciousness to us during our time there. We are still processing what happened, but I wanted you to know that it was an unforgettable experience. Not only did I visit Dad's grave, but I stood on the spot where he was killed; the lady who had been sitting next to him that night was with me, telling me everything that had happened. It was her husband who paid to have him killed. So many questions were answered, but more importantly we were able to witness the impact that my dad had on these people. There are over eighteen churches planted in the area where my parents worked—and even in the village where he was killed we sat with some believers and sang and read the Bible. As we were leaving the believers, they were witnessing to a neighbor lady.

It was abundantly clear that the Thai people loved him and twenty years later still miss him terribly. A number of them said they have never had such a bold witness since.

I can't thank you enough for making this happen. Perhaps some day I will be able to share more with you if you are ever in this area again.

Martina's letter deeply moved me. It brought closure to a daughter with regard to the death of her father, but it also opened a door to help her understand the immense impact of a life so faithfully lived.

"Many questions were answered." Yes, but many more will be answered when she sees her dad again in heaven.

Standing by the grave of her dad with the one whose husband had paid for the murder—what emotions must have surged through her heart! But Koos's grave is not his legacy. The eighteen churches are his legacy, and his memorial is on high.

God may not call many of us to pay for our faith with martyrdom. But we are called to see the gracious hand of a designing God in our lives. We are called to respond to God's nod. He holds the thread. He has given us his promise:

The design is beautiful. The promise is sure. The end result is profound. The answers will all be there. But the condition is clear; we must search for God with all our hearts.

Tying It All Together

As I was bringing this book to a close early one morning, I witnessed a vivid illustration of all that I have been trying to say. Sadly, it was not a pleasant experience.

I had just returned from an overseas trip during which I had bought my wife a beautiful necklace of semiprecious stones studded on a gold chain, each gem surrounded by zircons. The colors shone so beautifully that everyone who saw it said they wished they were the ones receiving it. I could hardly wait to present it to Margie. So at just the right moment, when the children were watching, I gave it to her. She loved it and asked me to tell her about the stones that adorned the necklace. That night we got to bed quite late.

I arose early the next day and went to the kitchen to make a pot of coffee. I was intending to begin writing the last chapter of this book. As I walked into the kitchen, I heard some crunching sounds. I looked in the direction of the commotion, and there, in the mouth of the puppy belonging to my daughter, was that beautiful necklace. Already it had been chewed into oblivion.

I must be honest. I just stood there, my eyes filling with tears. What could I do? This little representative of the canine world had absolutely no idea what she was destroying. Evidently she had stood on her hind legs and knocked the necklace down from the desk where my wife had left it. I had no rational way to tell this dog the damage she had done.

The puppy had taken a beautiful, elegantly designed piece of jewelry and treated it like a bone to chew on. It was not just that the dog destroyed something beautiful; worse, she had no understanding of the purpose of a magnificent piece of jewelry. I called my wife and showed her the remains. As she examined it, she thought it could be taken to a jeweler and repaired. (I have to admit that I wondered if there was a place to take the puppy as well. But for the sake of my daughter, I shall not head in that direction. Besides, the thought itself is unkind.)

Just think of the destruction of design in just one small piece of jewelry and how heartsick we feel about the loss. What, then, must be in the heart of God when we see no design and no purpose in our lives? What must God feel when we treat the crown of his creation as something to be consumed rather than something to be loved and admired with reverence? God intends to help each one of us live with his design in mind and not to trample underfoot his exquisite workmanship.

God wants none of us to perish. He left the ninety-nine sheep safely in the fold to go looking for the single lost one. Every one of God's creation, he wishes to preserve. His design for you is the best thing he has for you. Let God hold the threads so that you will someday see the beauty and the marvel he had in mind when he created you.

God holds the threads; you hold the shuttle. Move it at God's behest, and watch the making of something spectacular.

Text in this title was excerpted from The Grand Weaver by Ravi Zacharias which is available at your local bookstore.

978-0-310-26952-6